# He Persisted

## JAMES LESTER
## THOMPSON

LifeRich Publishing is a registered trademark of The Reader's Digest Association, Inc.

LifeRich Publishing books may be ordered through booksellers or by contacting:

LifeRich Publishing
1663 Liberty Drive
Bloomington, IN 47403
www.liferichpublishing.com
1 (888) 238-8637

ISBN: 978-1-4897-2370-3 (sc)
ISBN: 978-1-4897-2369-7 (e)

Print information available on the last page.

LifeRich Publishing rev. date: 07/01/2019

# He Persisted

**15 Men** *Who Put A* **Positive** *Impression*, *By* **Being A Good** **Example**, *On Many American Lives*

*This book is dedicated to my daddy, Mr. Theo Thompson Sr., a man who Persisted, even after retiring from his job, in working by doing various manual jobs to continue to provide for his family.*

*To some heroes and heroines of mine: Miss Evelena Myers, teacher, Mrs. Maude Pickett, teacher, Mr. Wallace Green, teacher, and Mr. Charlie Luckett, my favorite high school teacher.*
**– J.L.T.**

The word Persist means to continue strongly in an opinion or a course of action in spite of hard times, opposition, or failure. In other words, you have to keep going if you really want to reach your goal, whatever it may be in life. Sometimes your friends and some older people may tell you that you are not smart enough, and that you will never be a doctor, lawyer, engineer, or whatever your goal in life may be. Don't listen to these people. These fifteen American men sure didn't.

They persisted.

# Dr. Martin Luther King Jr.

After he had met a white boy, and they became good friends at the age of six, he soon noticed that they couldn't go to school together. He had to attend a school for African Americans, and his white friend had to attend the one for white children. Yet, he <u>Persisted</u> by continuing to get his education, becoming a Baptist minister, and later joining the Civil Rights Movement and was the leading activist. During this time, he fought hard to get laws that would do away with Jim Crow laws passed, so that black children and white children could go to school together, be treated equally in their pay for their work, and not be judged by the color of their skin but by the content of their character.

# Reverend Billy Graham

Mr. Graham turned to Christ seriously at the age of sixteen during a series of revival meetings in Charlotte, North Carolina. After completing his high school education, he attended Bob Jones College. He later had problems at this school and was almost kicked out. In addition, he was told by one of his teachers, "All you will probably ever amount to would be a poor country Baptist preacher somewhere out in the sticks." But he didn't let this negative talk bother him. Instead, he <u>Persisted</u>. And, by the late 1990s, he became known all over the world, speaking to live audiences of 210 million people or more in more than 185 countries and territories through various meetings, including BMS World Mission and Global Mission. He once said to a Ku Klux Klan member, "There is no scriptural basis for segregation. The ground at the foot of the cross is level, and it touches my heart when I see whites standing shoulder to shoulder with blacks at the cross."

# Thurgood Marshall

Was born in Baltimore, Maryland on July 2, 1908. His ancestors were slaves on both sides of his family. After completing high school a year early in 1925 with a B - grade average and later graduating from Lincoln University, he wanted to study law in his hometown law school, the University of Maryland School of Law. However, he didn't apply because this school, at the time, didn't allow black students to attend. But his legacy didn't stop there. Nevertheless, he _Persisted_ in furthering his education by attending instead Howard University School of Law, where he worked and studied harder than he had at Lincoln, and his views on discrimination were heavily influenced by the dean, Charles Hamilton Houston. In 1933, he graduated first in his class at Howard. Moreover, he later became Associate Justice of the Supreme Court of the United States from October 1967 until October 1991. Mr. Marshall was the Court's 96th justice and its first African American justice. He later became known as Mister Civil Rights.

# Medgar Wiley Evers

Although he had to walk twelve miles each day, whether it was raining or real cold, to attend segregated schools and eventually earning his high school diploma, he <u>Persisted</u> by continuing his education at the now Alcorn State University earning his Bachelor of Arts Degree. He went on to become the first field secretary for the National Association for the Advancement of Colored People (N.A.A.C.P.) for the state of Mississippi. Also, he became a leading activist in the Civil Rights Movement in Mississippi helping African Americans with voting rights, economic opportunities, getting into public schools and other facilities, and other changes in the segregated state of Mississippi.

# Mr. C.O. Chinn

He really loved the people of Madison County, Mississippi. Also, he wanted black people and white people to be treated equally. Despite the fact that he was threatened and told by the local sheriff on many occasions to get out of town before dark because of his Civil Rights work, he <u>Persisted</u> by continuing to put his actual life on the line by leading many Civil Rights marches, rallies, and meetings in the county. Mr. Chinn was responsible for helping black people to get into public places in Madison County, Mississippi and for making racial equality required across the county. Today he is known as the "Father of the Civil Rights Movement" in Madison County Canton, Mississippi. Once as a meeting was getting started at a local church, one of the Civil Rights workers stepped outside to ask him why he was sitting outside in his truck with a gun, and what he told the worker was as follows:

*"This is my town, and these are my people. I'm here to protect my people, and even if you don't like this I'm not going anywhere. So maybe you better leave."*

# James Meredith

Born June 25, 1933, he was a very important person during the Civil Rights Movement. After he was denied admission to the University of Mississippi, he was yelled and cursed at, life threatened, and told that no black people were allowed to attend their school by the students on the all-white campus. Yet, he Persisted. After getting help from President John F. Kennedy, Civil Rights leader Medgar Evers, and the federal government, he went on to become the first African American student admitted to the segregated University of Mississippi in 1962. With his persistence, he made it possible for future African American students to attend the school.

# Michael Jackson

Was from a musical family and had been performing since the age of four. He started out with four of his brothers as the lead singer of the Jackson Five, a band made up of just him and his brothers. Also, he was the youngest in the group, but he got to be the lead singer. It was extremely hard for him to be performing and singing at such a very early age. Yet he Persisted by winning every local talent show that he entered. And, by the time he was ten years of age, the band had a record deal. Later, he became nationally known all over the world for his singing and dancing talents. In addition, he was nicknamed the "King of Pop", and he was one of the most popular entertainers in the world and was the best-selling music artist during the year of his death.

# Elvis Presley

Inspired from an early age by his dream of becoming a big superstar in World music, Elvis Presley bought himself a guitar, and he practiced, and he practiced, and he practiced with it. By the time he entered the seventh grade, he began bringing his guitar to school on a daily basis. It was on these days that he played and sang during lunchtime, and he was often teased and called all kinds of bad names while he sang and was told by many of the other students that he wasn't anything but a kid who played hillbilly music. However, he didn't ever let these bad names bother him. Instead, he <u>Persisted</u> by continuing to sing and play his guitar and ignoring all the teasing to follow his dream of becoming a big superstar in World music. Later, he became one of the greatest singers and actors in the United States and throughout the world. Today, he is often referred to as the "King of Rock and Roll" or simply "The King".

# W.C. Handy

William Christopher Handy was born November 16, 1873, in Florence, Alabama. His father was the pastor of a small church, and he had very strict rules in his house. For example, his father believed that musical instruments were tools of the devil, and he didn't want them in his house. And, without his parent's permission, W.C. Handy bought his first guitar, and as soon as his father found out about the guitar, he made him take it back to where he had gotten it from. Yet, he <u>Persisted</u> by learning to play the cornet. But this time he kept this cornet a secret from his parents. Later, he joined several bands and orchestras learning to play several other instruments and traveling throughout the world, including places as far away as Cuba. Also, he became such a great musician of blues music until he became known as the "Father of the Blues".

# Booker T. Washington

Was born into slavery on a plantation in southwest Virginia, and his story could have ended there. Instead, he Persisted. After he and his family gained their freedom under the Emancipation Proclamation as U.S. troops came to their area, they moved to West Virginia, and it was here when Booker began very carefully to teach himself to read and attend school for the first time. He continued to get more education, and in doing so, he later became the first leader of Tuskegee Institute in Alabama. Also, he became an American educator, author, orator, and advisor to some presidents of the United States.

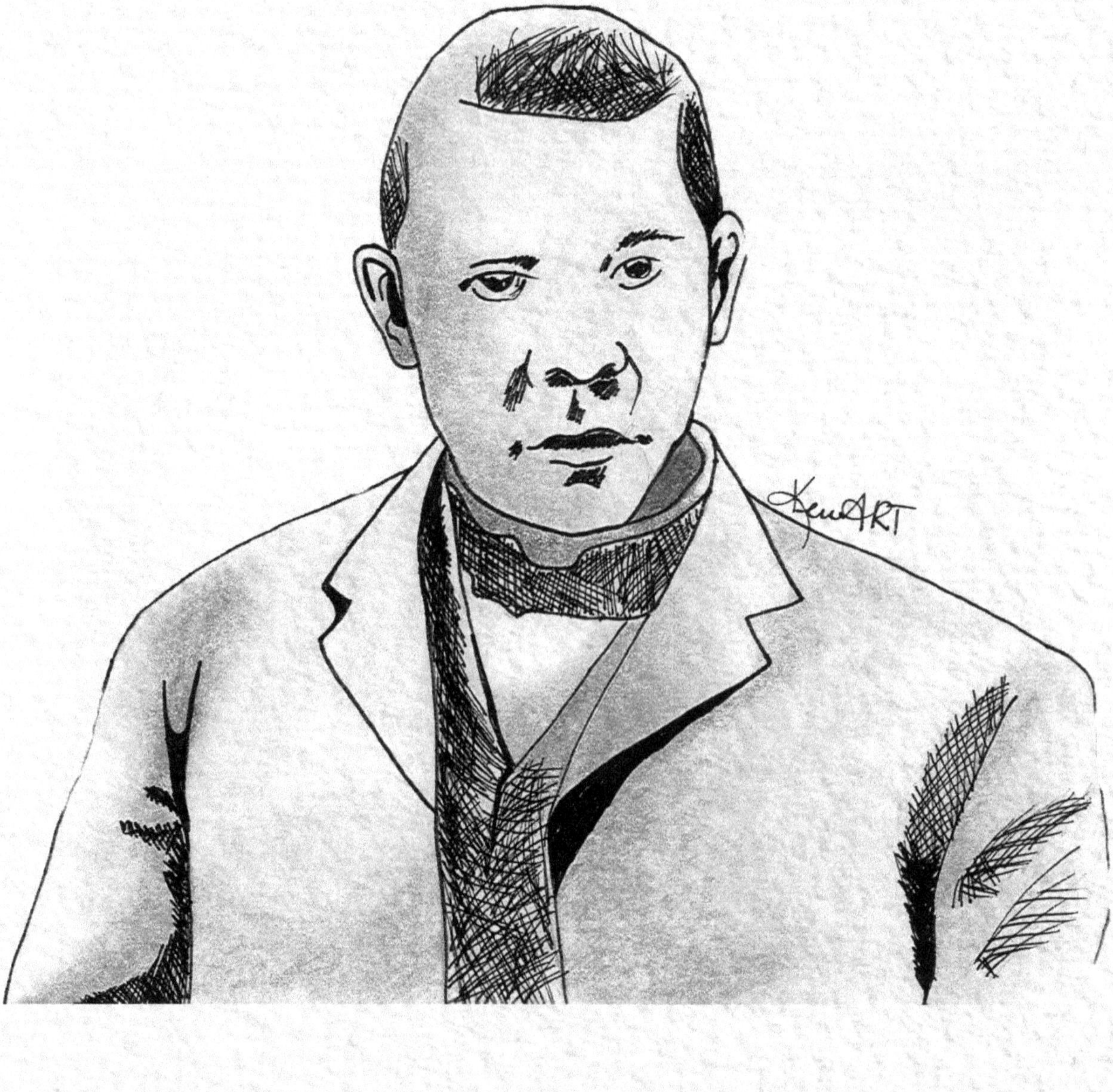
KenART

# John F. Kennedy

Despite having some form of dyslexia and severe and chronic back pain as a child, he <u>Persisted</u> by continuing to go after a good education. He attended Harvard University and served in the Navy during World War II where he was awarded the Purple Heart and the World War II Victory Medal. In addition, he served in both the House of Representatives and the Senate before becoming the 35th President of the United States in 1960.

# B.B. King

Riley B. King was born September 16, 1925, on a cotton plantation in Berclair, Mississippi. He was poor, and he had to work on this plantation and a few other cotton plantations. At the age of twelve, he bought his first guitar, and with the help of one of his cousins he taught himself how to play it. However, his story didn't end there. Instead, he <u>Persisted</u> in following his dream of becoming a great musician by continuing to play his guitar on local radio stations and in nightclubs from Memphis, Tennessee throughout America. Later, he became professionally known throughout America and the rest of the world as B.B. King, the great American blues singer, electric guitarist, songwriter, and record producer.

# Michael Jordan

While in high school, he developed a strong love for the game of basketball. But, when he tried out for the varsity basketball team during his sophomore year at Laney High School, he was told by the coach that at being only 5' 11" tall he was too short to play at that level. His taller friend, Harvest Leroy Smith, was the only sophomore to make the team. But he didn't let this stop him from trying. Motivated to prove his worth, he <u>Persisted</u>, ignoring what the coach had told him earlier and following his dream to become a great basketball player, he later became the star of Laney High School's junior varsity basketball team scoring forty points in many of its games. In addition, he went on to become one of the greatest basketball players in the world, winning six championships while playing with the Chicago Bulls basketball team. Also, he broke many records and earned many awards and honors. Today, he is retired. And, he is the principal owner and chairman of the Charlotte Hornets of the National Basketball Association (N.B.A.). Moreover, he is the third-richest African American, behind Oprah Winfrey and Robert F. Smith.

# Stevie Wonder

Although he was born six weeks premature and went totally blind a few weeks after his birth, his legacy didn't stop there. Instead, he <u>Persisted</u>. He began playing instruments at an early age, including piano, harmonica and drums. And, at the age of twelve he joined Motown Revue touring the "chitlin circuit" of theaters across America that accepted black artists. In 1963, he released his first major hit "Fingertips" at the age of twelve. Today, he has recorded more than thirty U.S. top ten hits and received thirty-five Grammy Awards, one of the most-awarded male solo artists, and has sold over 100 million records worldwide, making him one of the top sixty bestselling musical artists.

# Mr. Theo Thompson Sr., the author's father

Although he was told at a very early age that he had better hurriedly learn how to work, and despite the fact that he was raised on a plantation in the state of Mississippi in the early 1900s and wasn't allowed to go to school, he <u>Persisted</u>, becoming a great provider, once he became a grown man, for his wife and ten children by working hard in various manual labor jobs and not by selling illegal drugs or whiskey. Also, he educated two of his children beyond high school. One of his quotes that he often stressed to his sons is as follows:

*"Don't you ever sell drugs. A man don't have to sell dope and drugs to take care of his family. I never did it. And don't you all ever do it either."*

# A Little Advice For Students

Students, here are some very important tips for you to use to make sure that you will be successful in completing your education and reaching your goal in life. They are as follows:

1. Always obey your parents and teachers because they are the main people to go to for help and advice.
2. Pay close attention to your teacher while he or she is teaching the class.
3. If there is something about your lesson that you don't understand, ask your teacher to explain it to you again.
4. Study hard, so that you will know the lesson for each class and will score highly on all of your tests.
5. Each day after school, always make sure you do your homework first before going outside to play with friends.
6. Never give up on your goal. Just keep trying to reach it. These fifteen men in this book didn't. They Persisted.
7. Never say yes to drugs because you can easily go to jail or get killed.
8. Remember, while you are in school, that school is your main job, and there is work to do. And, never let anyone tell you what you can't become in life.
9. Always choose people who love to study and make good grades to be your friends, and you will do the same.
10. Always believe in yourself.

# A Little Advice For Teachers

As experienced educators, you probably already know or have already used this advice before. Also, you probably already know that many of your students come from a wide range of different backgrounds. For example, some students come from homes where there is a great deal of abuse. Some may come from single-parent homes. Others may come from homes where the importance of education isn't stressed to them at all. Therefore, these are the ones who really need encouragement. And, they really need you. In addition, you need to be their advocate. To be a good advocate, you need to encourage as much as you possibly can and support them in getting their education. Try to the utmost to make them feel loved and cared about at all times. There are a variety of ways to be a good student advocate. Nevertheless, here is just a few. And, they are as follows:

1. **Let the student know that you are there to listen**. For example, talk to them as much as you can, and let them talk to you keeping a good rapport with them.
2. **Allow the student to self-advocate**. For example, let the student and encourage the student to stand up for his or herself and make some decisions in problem solving.
3. **Be Persistent with the students**. For example, break longer assignments into smaller, more manageable ones, so that the students won't become frustrated at the thought of having to do a lot of work. Moreover, nothing succeeds like success. Set up activities where your students can shine, and they will want to continue the good feelings created by that success.

4. **Create safeguards**. For example, keep professional boundaries and do all you can to keep the student safe and from harm. Also, advise them to let you know if they see anything as suspicious or dangerous.

5. **Be a role model for the student**. For example, never use inappropriate conversation or profanity in the presence of your students. And, never come to work smelling like alcohol or drugs or dressed in an unprofessional and immoral way. And, last but not least, never date any of your students. In other words, showing your students love, encouraging them and supporting them in getting their education the best you can, and being the best role model and example that you can be for the students isn't the main way to be a good role model for your students; it is the only way.

CPSIA information can be obtained
at www.ICGtesting.com
Printed in the USA
BVHW011453220223
658998BV00004B/183